NEEDLE MAN

poems by

Edward McCrorie

with drawings by

Ivy Duffy

Also by Edward McCrorie . . .

Poetry

After a Cremation   (Thorp Springs Press, 1975)

"Asian and classical powers rumble and vibrate in these volcanic
poems, transforming their cool New England settings as they have
since Thoreau's day."

—*The Beloit Poetry Journal*

Translation

The Aeneid of Virgil (Michigan University Press, 1995)

"A phenomenal and masterly tour de force . . . a version of the Aeneid
translated line by line, remarkable for its fidelity to the original
not only in literal meaning, but also—equally important—
in spirit and sense."

—*The Join Association of Classical
Teachers Review* (London)

1999

Chestnut HIlls Press
a division of Brickhouse Books, Inc.
541 Piccadilly Road
Towson, MD 21204

Library of Congress Catalog Card 99-072340
ISBN 0-932616-64-X

*This book is a work of truth. All the names and events are real,
historically or imaginatively. Every resemblance to actual places and
people,both living and dead, is entirely by chance and by design.*

Most of these poems have appeared, sometimes in slightly different
form, in various magazines, which I am glad to acknowledge here:

Alembic: 'Spanish Steps'
The Beloit Poetry Journal: 'Needle Man,' 'Odysseus and
          His Sirens,' 'Under Story,' 'Poem Chain'
Delta Epsilon Sigma Journal: 'Catacomb' and 'Haiku: General
          Grant Grove'
Hyperion: 'Peregrine Watch' and 'Big Tree Talk'
Newport Review: 'Heathrow Taxi'
The Olney Street Anthology: 'Giving Away the Telescope,'
          'Your Foot,' 'Ghost Master,' 'On the Yangtse
          River at Dusk,' 'Variation on a Theme of Tu Fu,' 'Egg
          Drunk'
Poets Monthly: 'Toolmaker'
Rhode Island Review: 'Brief Bug Epic'
Spirit: 'Night Maring,' 'The Falls at Lauterbrunnen,' 'Bus 57'

A special thanks to Felix Mann for his books on acupuncture

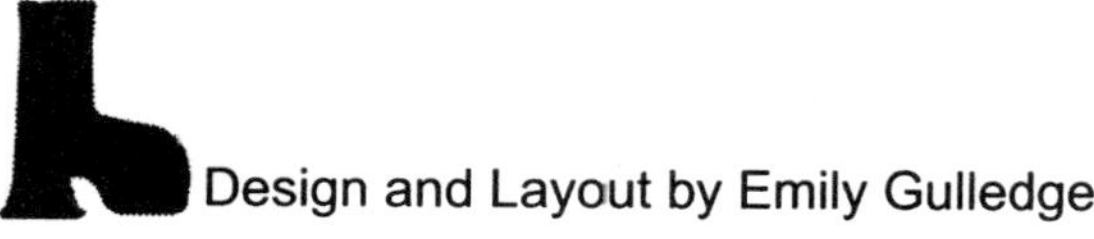
Design and Layout by Emily Gulledge

CONTENTS

Drawings

I
NEEDLE MAN

Needle Man

1

   'One way of regarding the structure of *I Ching* involves the family:
   parents (or grandparents) appear first in the work, followed by brothers
   and sisters, daughters and sons . . .'

Lying
down like a penned
white mouse, the die
of intestines rolling.

Someone says, 'Your father
had to lie down,'
kidneys and liver
drained of desire,

I picture the sky
a lover lying
on stripped coal, glittering
like slaves in his hold.

2

   'According to legend acupuncture was discovered accidentally
   on the field of battle, when arrow wounds in one part of the body
   affected organs in another part.'

Once there was a needle man
to fix these shivers

centuries ago in the sick
high of battle near Anyang,

when a wounded soldier saw
a line must run
from the heart to the hand,

lines of tender surface
and coursing depth:
a workable mystery,

the way a soldier's death
punctures a whole
dynasty collapsing.

3

'Emperor Huang Ti was probably the first to recognize the importance
of acupuncture, which then persisted as a medical practice into the
so-called Period of the Warring States . . .'

The emperor discovered health
in blades of the moon.
He swallowed wind-swords.

But emperors gave peace
to their people at spear-point.
They rode into battle on screams and erections

while their sages described
the superior man.

4

Bedridden,
slugs of arthritis

gunning you down, Grandfather,
where was that sickness?

Reeling from joint to joint,
swilling your fingers and spine,

minuscule gangs raided
your brain like stone.

I saw you once in daguerreotype,
Grandfather, riding a horse of copper
and carouseling Grandmother away.

You were no grandfather then:
you were a grown first son,

your tongue so close to your woman's ear
you might be whispering
my Mother.

5

> 'Her painful menstruation caused her to stay in bed and drugs were
> no help. I needled her on the inside of the knee once a month. After
> six treatments she was cured and has felt no pain for ten years.'

Faith is a slack muscle, Sister.
Faith is a firm thumb.

The man who can pedal the earth's organs,
pinpoint the chords of livers,
ride the golden meridians of your thigh,
Sister, and sound your anemones' depths:

the whole point of the Lord
telling Lazarus to rise:

whether six feet through or a membrane,
let the skin yield.

6

> 'And does the work of the mosquito resemble the acupuncturist's?'

An insect charms
coagulation from your blood.

She passes your headwaters
down to her children
wading in their pool.

When she has gone
your flesh rises,

you almost smile
the whole thing off.

7

'Perhaps Odysseus did more good than harm to Polyphemus . . .'

No man
could reach for a giant's eye
and cure him of leering with bare wood.

It must have been a needle man
who blinded all that killing

and showed him
how to bed down finally

with half truths.

8

Eldest daughter, in my nightmare
you diminish winds
and fork your only lung
in a candleless cenacle.

Someone says, 'Your grandmother
is better off now.'
In your last old home

you could not speak,
you could not keep quiet.

Before dawn your words and song
keep coming back,

your voice that tonified a household,
piano rolls, a popular waltz.

9

Illness returns,
a cancered rat,
chimps with cirrhosis.

Who can heal this healer?
Who is the battle film
maker without a stand-in,

pincered bugs feelering dust,
defenders who have never seen
the queen?

10

   'When Martin Luther King Jr. spoke . . .'

Causes go on lying
down, white mice
pinned with hypotheses.

My body in rags at thirty.
A needle man in black
purled some of that sinew,

stirring the lymph of
Brothers and Sisters,

lock your arms
and march down Main Street!

Open the windows, help me
to sweep up last night's sirens.

11

   'The ancient sages also taught that if a man withdrew before
   ejaculation he might satisfy a hundred women and lose none
   of his own substance.'

The ancient rods were silver.
Sunk in the flesh and deftly removed
they marched a hundred women off
to miracle cures of imbalance.

Rarely a womb contented itself
by giving birth to an emperor
hooked on design
of wounds that do not close.

Now your golden rod
enters a still pond
and the water divides
and stays there.

Go deep in the aging
flesh of this plane tree

and divine
the one woman.

12

    'Although St. George was intent on ridding the world of every
    evil, he reconsidered the evil . . .'

The dragon could not slaughter.
Sick as a lab experiment
his breath came hard.

A knight rode by,
he saw the bloodshot beast and he charged,
the dragon dodged too late:

the spear lanced him like a boil.
His nostrils cleared suddenly—
an oak caught fire!

He wanted to thank his healer.
But now the knight was gone
and wondering *Who am I?*

In time he shed his armor.
If someone lanced him now
his knightly nakedness would yield.

13

'And after the above and the below, Yang and Yin,
have been restored to balance . . .'

Reborn
a godwit,

aimed at crustaceans,
I've speared minnows alive.

Working lines of a marsh,
I know the above and below,

where they touch.

14

Georgiaville Pond:
your body divides when children
enter you like rods

and you remain whole.
Families form their circles
fragile as fingers

on the shore of a page.
They know what terminal pain
leaches down these hills.

Steady my hand.
Give us your aim.
The imaginable cure.

II

Giving Away the Telescope

For Charlie, Ivy and Their Daughters

You won't see everything now.
The black between Saturn
and its rings will look like a dot.
Lyra's nebula won't define itself.

But take your daughters west
of the city's haze on a summer night
and work their eyes.

Find the double star,
Albireo's blue and gold.
Trace the bloodlines of Sagittarius
down to the galaxy's heart.

Fix on Mars and tell them,
amazed when the planet drifts
from your field, it's their own
ground turning.

I'm not exactly handing over
craters of the moon here
losing a last golden
dusk with Venus.

Just letting go of a year
in my daughter's life. When you find her
drifting away from nine or ten
and blurring in far-off twelve,

the lenses will need more dusting.
You'll often stay indoors.
The stars are simply there again.

Haight Street Later

The smell of mint and sassafras.
A man stands up
in the Haight Street teahouse
chanting

I am Yahweh

and remember brothers
today is the Lord's day.

No one contributes.
I'd like to check his claims,
the man has needled me,

but he's down the block already
looking for a better
Sinai.

Jason's Woman

You kept surrounding me with names.
A cat called Juno, Nymphs in the tub,
incense from Saba. I half imagined
halved lambs on the table.

I kept wishing away the haze,
the ether from your lips.
Your hair was enough saffron,
your breast unolympian.

You kept a votive eye on the nights
I tried without much hope
to change it all
back into basic metal.

Haiku

1 Appletree

Seed: apple blossom
pollen so numberless
my neighbor calls it dust.

2 Sundial

He needles the sky
and earth moment: the gnomon's
finger and shadow.

Night Maring

Our stitching and unstitching has been naught.

Yeats

A Gloria climbs for the adzed voussoirs
of Beauvais cathedral
and sinks back down. Purple vestments
freckle the huge womb,

a nave not done. The bishop dreamed,
mad as a full moon's mare,
but the hooves got stalled. Limestone vaults
are chunks of a Gothic cadaver.

The horse is trunkless. Workmen plastered
the sanctuary ceiling:
it fell in 1284, the year they call
the end of the Middle Ages.

*

Late that night I'm ferried to England
recalling a boyhood dream
of falling. Whacking the poplar's branches,
hitting the ground so hard

I emerge in China. The call of a Beauvais
cleric rings in my ears,
challenging prisoners: Climb to the ceiling,
fit those keystone clouds together

and win your freedom. A man tries
and he topples. I fall through the floor,
through hell, and I break ground
on the world's underbelly.

People in old Peking smile
at my story. The Emperor asks,
Are you surprised the sky
was underneath you?

We'll go back through the soil
and emerge in Europe
where half of a church
will still be waiting.

Brief Bug Epic

Book I

Moths are born already crushed.
They're sixty percent or better
rag content.

Book II

Ants winding: a fat-free snake.
They welcome clear work assignments.
Do not try to stuff an ant.

Book III

A tick is a bit of mis-
placed emphasis
in my hair. Insis-

ting I'm a drinkable giant.

Book IV

Lovebugs swarm on the highways!
Clotting motel windows,
blind-siding the tankers:

the chemical company's powerless.
Spanish moss is learning
already to live with them.

Book V

Those who like to munch
in a cat's ear might
as well be mites.

Book VI

Butterflies are clever replies
to moths' questions.

Days keep answering,
nights keep asking.

Book VII

Dragonflies are quick
and elusive as Emily
Dickinson stanzas

or lovers.

Book VIII

Desert locusts like to feed
on honey and wild people.

Never ask a locust
about sabbaticals.

Book IX

Wasps can build an octogenarian
breast whose milk
puts on wings.

Book X

Bees predigest the honey
of night-time apple snacks.
They curl and snooze to perfection.

III

After Calling the Pest Man

He's here at dusk, shouldering bags
of powder and tools. The bees, he tells me,
are sleeping now. A bush sags
under its lilacs close to the nest.

The sky weakens. Grass turns black
where he stands at the northeast corner,
checking partitions. He aims gas,
the gun like a bellows, his face masked,

and he pumps hard, filling the wood.
No angry buzz or screaming inside.
A flashlight spots no bee blood,
only a few fall out of the cloud,

fewer circle poorly away and
bump into leaves in the dark,
muttering stories of loss
the lilacs can hardly believe.

Rome Elegies

1 Catacomb

A young Chinese led us down
into stone blindness. Niches appeared
sucked from the walls, their bones

and icons missing. The guide gestured:
a child was whisked from that crypt.
Treasureless tombs.

He led us back upstairs
into sun blindness. Palm pirouettes,
a herd of elephant-ears,

the eucalyptus musk. He pointed
at sky and told me Venus is *there*
if your eyes can gather her light.

2 Spanish Steps

Red-eyed windows glint at signoras.
Keats died across the square.
I head for a bar called BYRON.

Wine shushes the would-be doctor
and poet. Day-old arthritic steel,
infarcted churches and temples.

I won't climb the steps tonight.
Deep in the bar somebody coughs
but TB's dead of course.

I have no pills or patches.
Why do you keep on hacking?
My wine won't change your blood.

3 Bus 57

Back to the Tiber Hotel at rush-hour
in Rome, hundreds of women shoppers
and glare, like a white wine, filling each dip.

A child clings to his mother's blouse
when the bus lurches, fingers ripple
in hairshine, faces ricochet

off glass and aluminum, specters of doubles:
the green ghost of our whole company
stops in a window of Cim's.

Dozens of swifts are circling above us.
They home on thousands of flies,
their permanent, edible dome.

Your Foot

Keep a close eye on your foot.
That's where it comes from first.

Even your teenaged heel
won't tickle under that crust.

My Mother used to snip
my Grandmother's jaundice toenails

and off they would fly like
beetles, thwacking the window.

I was young but I knew.
I kept my distance.

Corns and blisters three years old
turn grey and shed,

even a pointed arch
falls eventually.

Socrates' brain was warm
but he drank that plant

and the jailer pressed his foot:
Can you feel that? No, he said.

The quiet spread like a lifting
skirt to his calves and knees.

Egg Drunk

The dairy man smiles when I ask
for a quart of the Christmas eggnog,
thick as his forearm. He says last night
he drank himself stupid with that stuff
and dreamed of a scramble of blondes.

With enough yolk-yellowed cream
maybe I'll dream of my Father tonight
fixing the beige 'forty-nine Ford
in the socket black of the old barn,

the car blued by its smoke when he moved it,
hens reclaiming the dark behind us --
Gwendolyn, Charity and Felicia

cackling, laying for Grandma,
the nutmeg-speckled yellow and white
dribbling my mouth in the morning.

Under Story

'But Bobby kept on looking at her sadly and
explained that it wasn't during the day—that
she was mean at night, when he was asleep.'

Cortazar

The guide knelt down.
This creeping jenny's voice
he said is faint,

not like forest canopy,
crowns of oaks with a loud
line to the sun.

Late that night I heard
a jenny's whisper: *Let me
tell you an under story,*

*chill your roothairs
and help you live
with pieces of light.*

I said, I'm here,
I'm listening.

*

Back in the wildlife refuge
our guide's botanical eye
was ranging widely,

drinking uncut milkweed,
wondering where a daisy left him.

I watched her syllables form,
a gold ore
in the dark that night,

far-off language calling
the way a mother calls from childhood:
words, not only words.

     *

Now the guide was rambling,
figuring oaks are a green sky
for the skunk cabbage.

Birches, anchored flotillas:
shucking seed and mulch.

A current of air was bending
the leaves of *peregrina veronica*—
she won't keep still.

That night in my room
a painted trillium beckoned
and told me without a word

You're my Zeus:
rain

     *

No one, the guide told us,
wants a swamp naturally.

Dry in August,
a thousand blue-eyed berries
blinked in the dust.

At three in the morning
sleeping poorly,

a black-eyed susan under
stated it:

I am the witch
who'll wind your sheet
in chocolate and gold.

Barely audible
sound that a mother makes
when a boy is facing

the whole of sleep.

*

The guide found a cremation.
Charred understory,

a bird lamely tending
what looked like an oven.
She went inside as if to die

and nested instead.
Her children can only fly
from the ground up.

I followed a sweet cicely
rising at dawn:

Enjoy your canopy light.
The scorpion sky you invent.

Take my knowledge too:
your friends are my leaves' veins,
caterpillar prey

who amble back from a grave or belly
with strange under
stories.

Imagine you go dow
to a pupal dream

and emerge wingtip

Poem Chain

I see you've kept some careful records,
calling the grubs hardly
syllables at all. A meal,
though, for the starling.

And she, for all her squabbling,
a pure morsel for the mother
owl, who feeds the tender
eyes to her young.

Your notes are thorough. In time
a woman (could that be you?)
snares and stews the owl.

She lifts a spoon to her man's lips:
an eye is floating there like a split
doubloon . . . Could we stop now?

You smile. I sip.

IV

Peregrine Watch

Your shift: you're stuck on the cliff
three hours. Talk and you scare off
parent birds. The nestlings starve.

The falconer sees things different.
Dangle a moon in spring,
leave him alone like a lover

and down he'll go with the young.
Their eyes will be stitched shut.

So you're on guard.
Wondering whether the birds know
in some bird way or care . . .

You've seen the biggest raptors
empty the nest, flushed
at the slightest word,

a burst of escaping wing
at the first chance.

Big Tree Talk

1 Haiku: General Grant Grove

Real trees who outlive
imaginary gardens,
how can my leaves last?

2 Utah Nightmare

Stuck in the wrong motel
on a dry state line,
a roomful of chopped sequoias

dropped from the train by men
wanting to show off the West
and share generations of growth

with Boston family men
who cannot believe their eyes
and label it all a hoax.

3 Great Grandparents

Dozing in the family car
re-entering New England.
A reddish bear mother

took me though mounting snow
searching for great
grandparents' warmth.

She saw the grove where lightning
had pottered a still live tree
six hundred Novembers

before I was born.
We arranged ourselves
in the fire-wrought urn.

Swiss Airs

1 The Falls at Lauterbrunnen

for Rodney

You drove us hard through over-land
to see another falls.
Up close, you said.

The sky scaled like yarrowstalks,
whitewater tongues flicking
the Jungfrau's withers.

We stumbled along below.
Needles of water stitched my face
and you asked, Now was it worth it?

To see a river fall without loss
of power or aim: to be stuck
with my own sprouting in your rain.

2 Flying

Flicked from a green finger at dawn
our toy's pilot is Father Bochensky,
chainsmoking at seventy,
chaintalking and rattling

the airplane south past Monte Rosa
and Mont Blanc. His eyes fixed
on the pure forms.

I tried to follow the side-
windering Rhone below me. He followed
ridges marching in perfect step

to where the last film was purged
and Plato rose to deny
and avow the deep blue God.

Heathrow Taxi

Radio noise at dawn.
Bomb threats at the airport.
The artery ticks on my arm:

it's time to be leaving for Rome.
The driver likes cold rain:
he spent years in the Amazon

stepping aside for jungle bugs
as big as doubloons,
green herons I half

imagine needling the brown
hips of passing utility poles,
thighs of leaf spread on the guardrail.

Never a meter click on the River,
he says at the terminal,
time is your own.

Bags gaping like circus
jaguars. Rays turning
our insides out.

Odysseus and His Sirens

for Picasso and his painting

1 Noise

I'm lashed in place and my ears
are labyrinths ringing,
cochleas multiplied,

legs locked and running
away, my head is looted
by visions of fisharms

and flukey legs,
generations of bees' honey:
it's no use bolting,

another world of jeweled
barbarity greens my wrists
and I'm prize

litter of shells, my eyes
bone white as their own.

2 Faces

Fleshtone runoff.
Salt and Midi sun
adore this color: film
goddesses cook in a week.

The cloth goes too. Museum
canvas and oak begin to flow,
a sort of uncoagulation.
Sandy trickles of stone.

Ah, but it's summer! Time
for a painter to seize ripeness.
Until they quarrel. Anger
rings in his ears

and the mauves mix in his head:
he cigarets her cheek.
She's flesh, she burns.
And wonders if genius

is only a short-order cook,
palette and ripeness
down to nothing
but surface cooling.

3 Sleep Walking

Smoke and paint are a spectacle
of myself. They call this place
The After Burner.

Cronies are here:
McManus talks about treeing
the army jeep again

and we all laugh. A woman
tells me, I am Circe.
Right, I tell her, and I'm
a purple heart on Zeus.

She smiles: What if you sailed
too close to a siren song?
I smile: I'd keep both pistols cocked.

Always prowling, she says, for a shootout.
Your world can sing with an over
and under spirit: you'll keep
piddling with plan buildings.

Now she's needled me. I'm asking,
What was your name again?
She sneers: Look at this place,

your carbonated tongue,
fingers clutching their straws.
Let your hands go,

blind as a Greek oar!
Sail in your sleep.

4 Fish Story

Under water the eels are waiting.
You and the nightfish wheel
like zodiacal signs.

Cast your eyes like lures
back to the surface, now a sky.
You know that loving every

siren song is impossible.
And necessary. Every axil
of finger and fluke

that trebles your ear, the schools
of bluefish hitting all
the joints in Scorpio,

the rare bowhead whale
tilting Polaris. Watch
with the eyes of a fish-god:

no one's the one who got away
as far as Antares winking,
playing with distance vision,

the human child
and the fish child lost
and found to the naked eye.

Toolmaker

He takes a chair in the front row
with his poor hearing. The eyes
are a fine micrometer's wink.
His job ended. The man is seventy.

Talking down to his knowledge and skill,
I am uneasy. Chalk like a bird's
bones on the blackboard:
Beowulf's funeral, Lear's daughters.

His finger looks for a quoted verse.
A classmate helps. He sometimes dozes
or misses a class. From sickness? No,
his family forgot to prod him out.

He takes a chair for the final exam,
his pen unsteady. Then it comes down,
hard as a stylus, and cuts
the new syllables.

V

GHOST MASTER:
A CHINA SEQUENCE

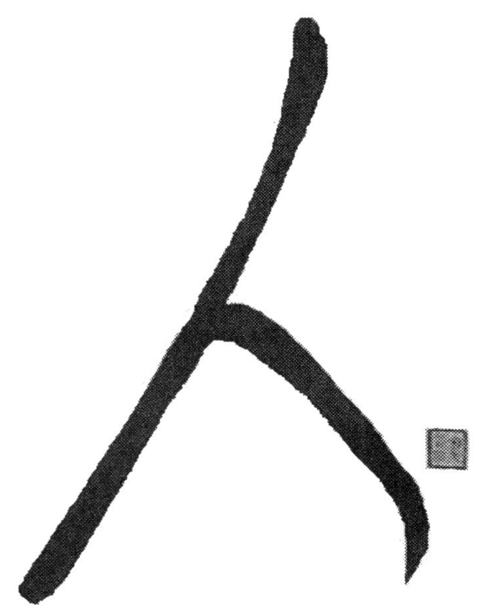

Ghost Master: A China Sequence

Imperial Stroll

Hour by hour
people become

smaller in Shanghai's
Ming Garden,

arms limp
in July heat,

vague as the thin
goldfish and bamboo

paling under
the water, I lose

flab like a common
working Chinese.

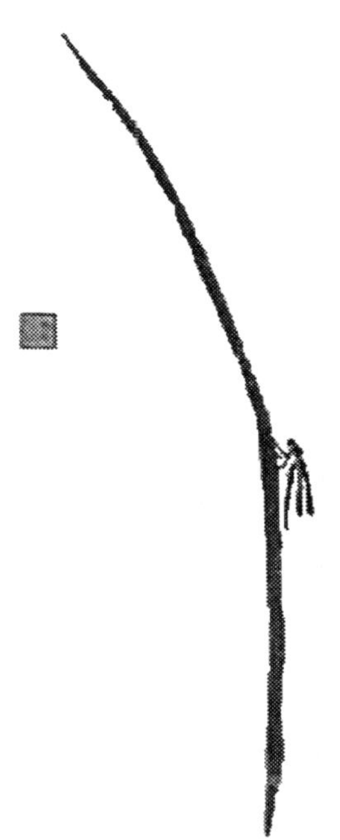

The Origin and Development of Unreal Aninals

"Don't be frightened by the plant sculptures at the
entrance to the Nanjing Zoo. They're not real dragons."

—local China guide

"In a moment the nine-fold true dragon emerges."

—Tu Fu, "A Song of a Painting,"
translated by David Hawkes

1

A tiger stalked each bronze.

In abstract Shang design
(not yet tongues or tails)
a Zhou craftsman saw
the stretching of body:

bronze by bronze
neck and claws extended,

the mouth's raw-meat heat
finally whispering *dragon*.

2

The old duke laughed
at unreal animals.

Unable to sleep
he saw the air
undulate one night

and a tongue
so warm in his ear!

The children who made
dragons real
behind a screen

smiled and took their bows.

3

Gold slashing a jade bush:
nine-foot tigers are still
in Sungary River country.

This one's snuffing its steel bars.
Up close I caught a whiff
of his dead-meat breath.

The scales and wings
were gone from his back.
Prey and terror
hosed from the cage,

only the hide a quiver
of ancient fire.

Short Train Song
(Shanghai-Nanjing)

A hundred miles of farmland. Green
tubs of rice. A man
alone among lean
stalks, the sky wet as the land.

The China passion for plain
life, green tea or plain
water, rice porridge that's more water
than rice, boys bare in the water.

Beijing Quatrain

A master has carved in jade
a pair of old sages, seen
among clouds of ghostly jade,
the whole inside a tangerine.

Long Life

Cranes in a Beijing zoo
with an aura of old age
are fed with care.

The Wall to the north,
dragoning stone miles,
may be deathless too,

like the weeks and months
of Beijing kindergartners,
their mothers away in the south,

they dance in a screechy circle,
asleep or awake each night
in cribs by the classrooms.

My dream looked ageless too.
Underground bureaucrats
preened their tweed

like tall birds after a meal.
To them it was nothing
but one more day.

The Devil Catcher

A Guilin artist painted
the old man with singed
blue hair, a squint in his eye
and grandmotherly dugs.

The Devil Catcher. He wandered
the fields and helped farmers
through Han Dynasty nights.
He brought each devil to bay,

arresting the spirit's eye
first with a sit-down game:
lines and squares the devil
presumed he could read

but lost track of and lost.
So danger passed like a small
hour. At dawn the farmer
remembered wisps of cloud.

No one dares to roll up
the scroll now, devil and catcher
alike, those hands, that muttering
sack to take back home.

Remembering Li Bai

You first gave character
to Xiling Gorge in Tang times,
working song from the stone
that stayed intact.

Workers chanting together
are shrinking the hill this year,
one song at a time. Ground
remembering something

of yin-laced dark is yielding
to picks and shovels. Heights
come down for a spread of homes,
a leveling China,

the need for far more paddies
to plant. Where crags were once
there are airs, new sky, old ghosts
haunting us both nights.

On the Yangtse at Dusk

A boy on the riverbank
chopsticks the last of his rice,
oblivious of strata behind him,
a cliff's cache of millenia.

I'm down with a Western bug.
Small as the semi-tropical
rain or the half stroke
of a sampan punter,

I swallow my Chinese pills,
evergreen extract. The river's
brown muscle relaxes.
I doze off seeing

the winged mountain soar
into dragon country, scaled
thundercloud coiling, every
tongue on fire on the ridge.

Half waking
I lose count of the times
a junk fisherman casts
lines for four-inch eel.

Variations on a Theme of Tu Fu

Gazing at Tai-Shan Mountain once
you saw a green so hard and high
you wrote of the god who judged the dead,
his air as thin as a grandmother's sigh.

You wanted to stand on the peak yourself
For the best vision of sky and land.
In a village north of Guilin now
I'm watching mountain-like pillars of sand

sheathed in green thrust from the earth
as though they could choke the cowering sun.
Bone-hard dragons from under the world
that roil blue fields and clouds on the run.

I've wanted to plunge beneath that surge,
go down to the bed of the karst range
for a better view of the sky below
and maybe a god the dead still know.

Wu Han Riddle

Kept in a jar
in a Chinese doctor's house

I'm little or nothing
but skin

helping to heal
a murmuring heart,

not much more,
until he opens the jar

and I fly out
and around in lopsided circles,

birtz into chairs, your shoulder,
my see-through wings

and bass-string voice
bringing a smile,

needling
family and friends.

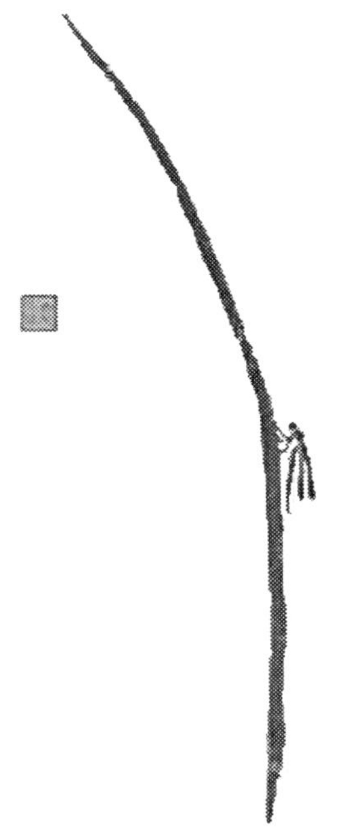

Ghost Master

In scroll after scroll he squats or walks
like a wizard, bearing a jumble
of crates and vessels, weighed with long-gone
Taoist ghosts, planters, masons
and death-blue poets from leveled mountains,
mothers who died after their children.
I've seen him hang from a gallery wall
and tighten the lids on dragonfly specters,
watch his wraiths of arachnids at night,
gathered at streams, on the heights of gorges,
the wisps of doctors who needled a Qing
emperor, Han ladies with smoke-thin
songs of a braided and broken love.

The jumble grows each year. More
to be mastered when men like Sun are lost,
or a tiger bloodline frays in the woods.
When Chongqing workers cannot escape
to the air-raid shelter in time, and every
dead weight is acting as though
it's alive, a mutter of too-close thunder.

Now the aging master, a picture
of sagging breasts and a lingering smile,
takes on the look of a heaped coolie,
knees bending under a silkworm
sack. He shudders carrying older
stacked-up spirits, Yin and Yang
in a muted duet, Weapons and Wealth
rusting already and Chance himself
playing his oldest role, mere luck.

Today the master's a railyard worker
stooped beneath his luggage and heat.
And that old woman I saw shouldering
too much fruit in a river town.
She set it down and sat in the shade,
then lifted the bags and walked again.

Waking in a Chinese Mansion

Stumble from bed at night
dragging the scales and claws
of a dream to the john,

amazed at the size of my rooms:
am I rich in China now?
A privileged Party member?

The night-light snickers.
Gaining weight like a Buddha,
darkness blocks me and grins,

spooking my hand and wraith
of a penis. I belong
and don't belong in my own house.

About the Author...

Edward McCrorie was born in Rhode Island, took his Ph.D. in English at Brown in 1970, and is now Professor of English at Providence College. He's published his poems in many journals and anthologies, and he regularly presents his work, both poetry and translation, to a wide variety of audiences. He continues to work out of a deep and broad matrix that includes ancient and modern writers, Western and Eastern culture, the four elements and the four winds. He also has four daughters (by chance, or maybe by the guiding Chance of the ancient Chinese), and he now lives with his second wife, Beatrice Beebe, in New York City and Providence.

He welcomes e-mail at mccrorie @providence.edu.

About the Artist...

Ivy Lyew Duffy was born in China and lives in Providence, Rhode Island with her husband, Charles; they have two daughters. In addition to her art, she has taught French and Taiji.